HOW THE SUN MOVES WATER AROUND THE EARTH

by **Molly Bang**
& **Penny Chisholm**

illustrated by **MOLLY BANG**

THE BLUE SKY PRESS
An Imprint of Scholastic Inc. • New York

RIVERS OF

SUNLIGHT

NEPTUNE

URANUS

SATURN

JUPITER

MARS

I AM YOUR SUN.
My energy warms your days.
I light up your world.

But of all my planets,
only one is teeming with **LIFE:**
your Earth. Why?
Because it is covered with water—H_2O—
always moving, always changing, from liquid
to solid to vapor and back again.

Together, water and I
give **LIFE** to your blue planet,
and to **YOU.**

EARTH

VENUS

MERCURY

Almost all of Earth's water
is in your salty seas.

To you,
the oceans seem very deep.
But they are actually just
a thin, thin film covering
most of your planet.

Look! If ALL Earth's water were rolled into a ball, the ball would only be THIS big → compared to the whole Earth.
A ball of just Earth's *fresh* water would only be THIS big, → and most of that is locked away as solid ice or water buried underground.

What's left?

← Just THIS tiny bit of fresh water.

And yet this tiny bit is enough to keep ALL life on land alive. How?

Because water moves— it cycles!

And so it is used again and again and again.

Drink a glass of water. Feel it flow into your body.
Most of your body is made of water.
Water carries food and oxygen to every cell
and helps keep your temperature just right.

The water you drink stays inside you for a few days
and then travels on, flushing your wastes away.
Just as water flows and cycles inside you,
it flows and cycles around your Earth—
keeping ALL life alive.

Where did your water come from?

Where is it going?

What keeps it moving?

I do! I, your sun.

I lift water from the salty sea
by warming the ocean's surface waters.
See how my heat makes the H₂O molecules
jiggle, jiggle, jiggle until they pop into the air,
leaving their salt behind.

That's EVAPORATION!

Liquid water becomes a gas: water vapor.

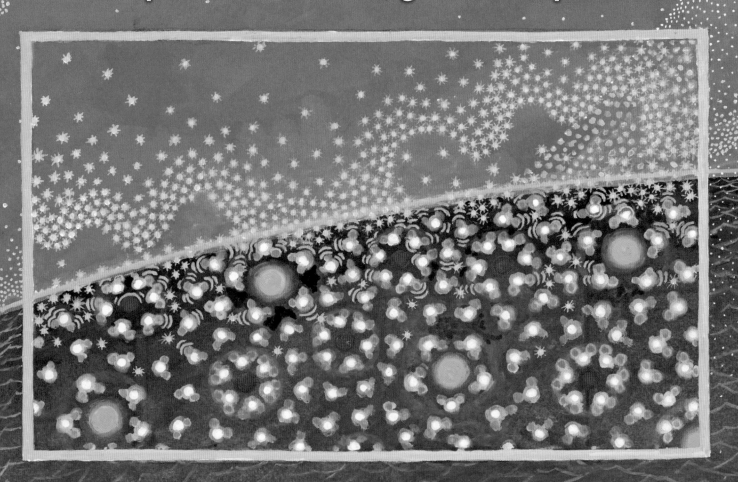

The molecules of
pure, *fresh* water vapor
FLOAT UP . . . . UP . . .

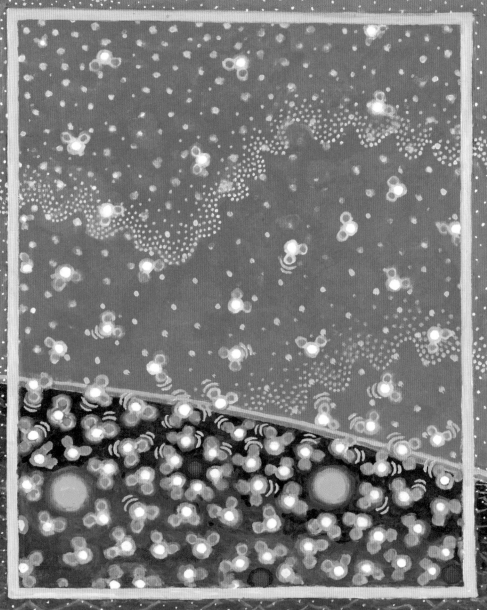

. . . AND SPREAD OUT.

They join a cocoon of water vapor that
envelops your whole Earth.
This cocoon catches some of my light energy
and helps keep Earth's temperature
just right for LIFE.

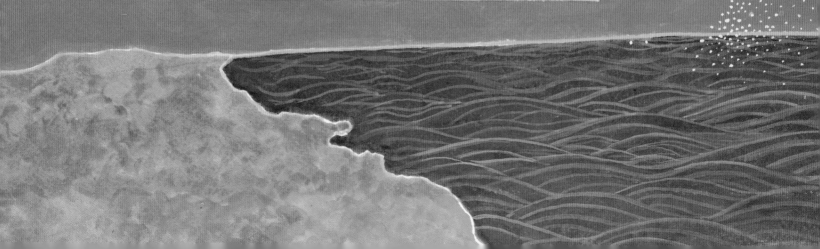

Some of the water vapor rises even higher, to
cooler layers of the atmosphere. When a molecule
of the vapor catches a speck of dust, suddenly
millions more grab hold, to form one drop.

Water vapor becomes a liquid once again.

Drops collect in clouds.

They grow larger, heavier,

until they pour out of the

sky as rain or snow, and

fall back into the sea.

But some of the water vapor above the sea . . .

. . . joins a river of water vapor flying through the sky.

My winds blow the river
across the sky toward land.
Now rain and snow fall there.

Snow piles up on mountaintops
each winter. In the warmth
of spring, it melts and flows
with fallen rain to streams,
rivers, and lakes.

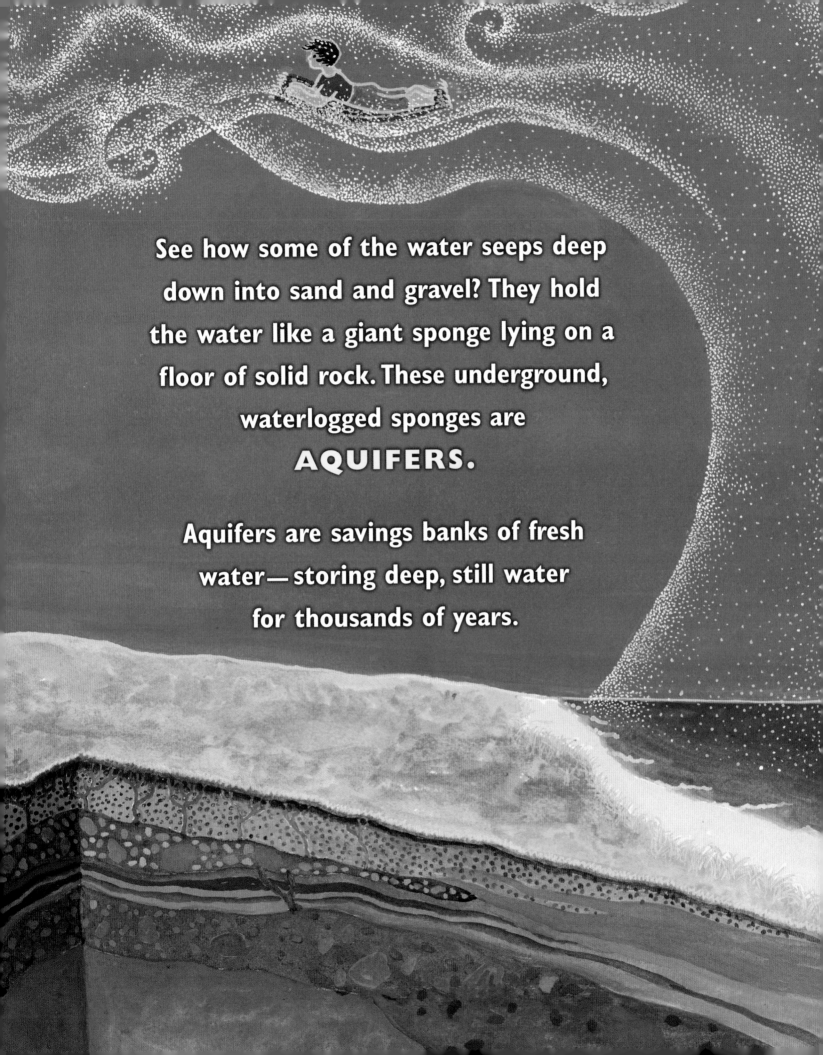

See how some of the water seeps deep
down into sand and gravel? They hold
the water like a giant sponge lying on a
floor of solid rock. These underground,
waterlogged sponges are
AQUIFERS.

Aquifers are savings banks of fresh
water—storing deep, still water
for thousands of years.

Above them,
I keep water moving, moving.

I shine my light on lakes, rivers,
and soggy soil.

Again, water evaporates
into the air.

I shine my light
on trees and plants.

They draw up water from the ground and use
my light to photosynthesize—building more
plants, which feed ALL living things on Earth.

As they photosynthesize, the plants
pump water vapor into the air.

It rises up to join the giant river in the sky.

My winds push the flying river, so rain and
snow fall on mountains, prairies, forests,
and deserts, nourishing plants there.

**And so water cycles
round and round, over
and over and over again.**

What would happen
if I did NOT move water?

There would be no rain, no rivers . . .
no LIFE on your blue planet
if I did not move water.

And I move a LOT of water!

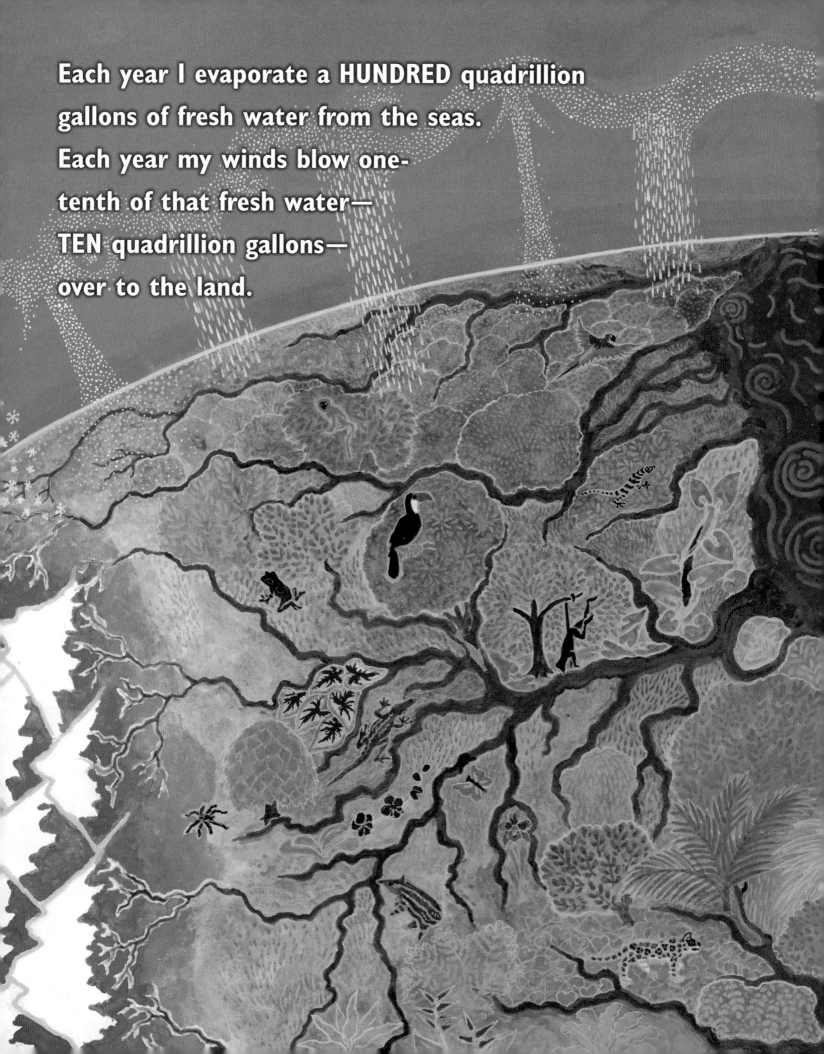

Each year I evaporate a HUNDRED quadrillion
gallons of fresh water from the seas.
Each year my winds blow one-
tenth of that fresh water—
TEN quadrillion gallons—
over to the land.

The rest falls
back into the sea.

BUT—
if I keep moving fresh water from the seas
to land, why don't the seas get saltier and saltier?
And why don't they eventually *dry up*?

Because each year the rivers of the world
deliver TEN quadrillion gallons of fresh water
back to the seas, replacing what was lost.

I keep water moving, cycling from
sea to air to land and back again.
I keep the cycle in balance.

And I also cycle water IN the seas.

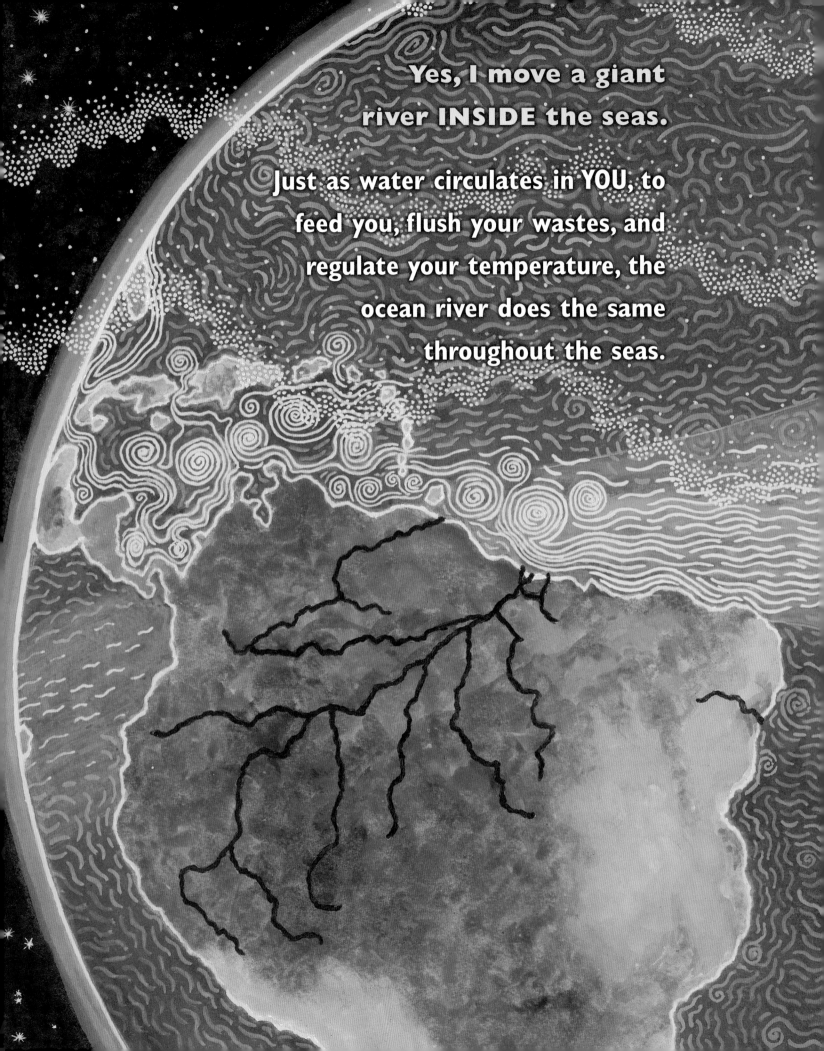

Yes, I move a giant
river **INSIDE** the seas.

Just as water circulates in **YOU**, to
feed you, flush your wastes, and
regulate your temperature, the
ocean river does the same
throughout the seas.

HOW?

My light heats your Earth's
equator steadily all year long, so
the surface water there stays very warm.

My winds help move a wide current of that
warm water west, until . . .

the current bounces against land—the Americas!—
and curls back into swirling eddies.

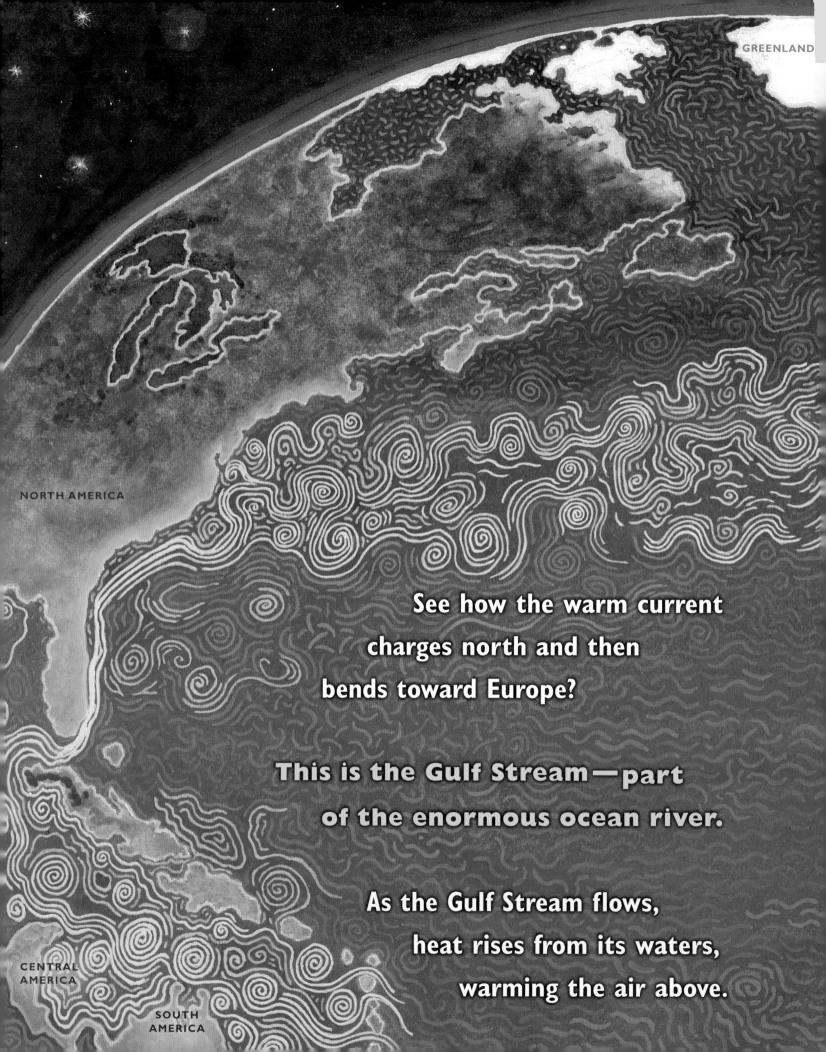

GREENLAND

NORTH AMERICA

See how the warm current
charges north and then
bends toward Europe?

This is the Gulf Stream—part
of the enormous ocean river.

As the Gulf Stream flows,
heat rises from its waters,
warming the air above.

CENTRAL
AMERICA

SOUTH
AMERICA

EUROPE

AFRICA

My winds blow
that warm air
over land, where it
heats the land itself.

If the Gulf Stream didn't
flow, winters in Europe
would be MUCH colder!

As it lets go of its heat, the Gulf
Stream's water cools. In the far north,
some of it freezes into solid ICE,
squeezing its salt out into the sea.

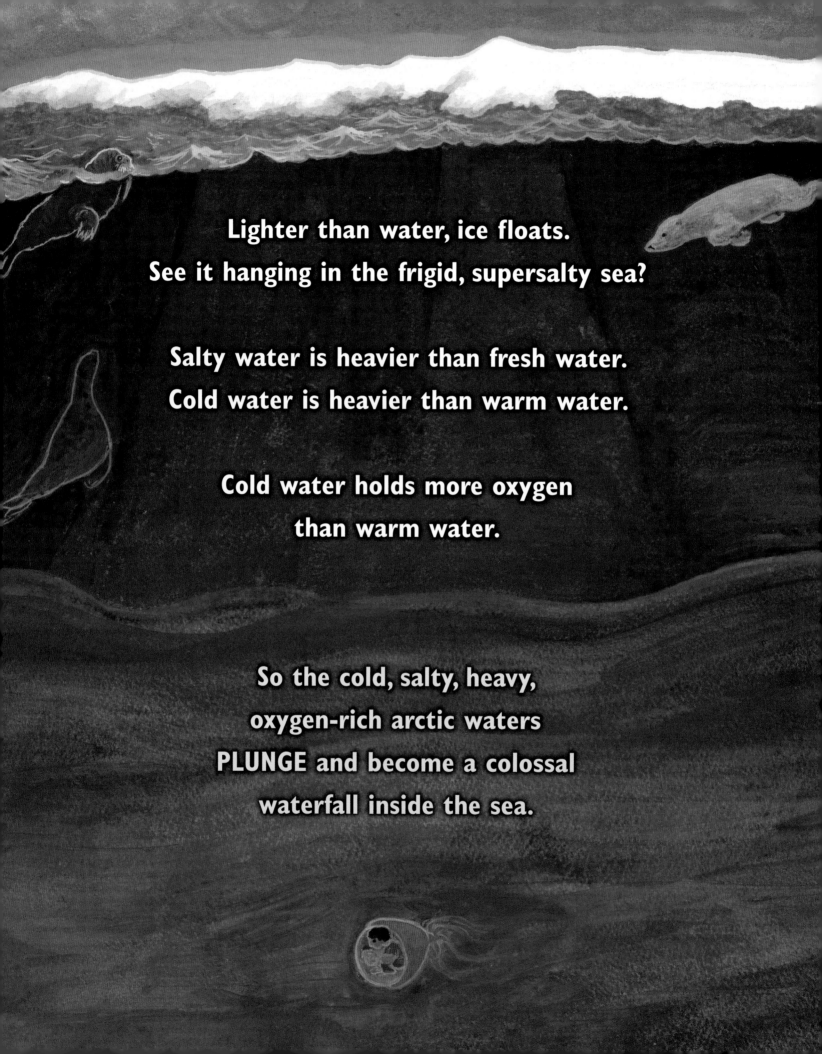

Lighter than water, ice floats.
See it hanging in the frigid, supersalty sea?

Salty water is heavier than fresh water.
Cold water is heavier than warm water.

Cold water holds more oxygen
than warm water.

So the cold, salty, heavy,
oxygen-rich arctic waters
PLUNGE and become a colossal
waterfall inside the sea.

TWO MILES deep
it plummets—driving
the giant river along
the ocean floor.

This massive artery
of water is the great
Ocean Conveyor Belt.

The Conveyor Belt snakes
through the deep dark
ocean, delivering oxygen
to deep-sea creatures and
gathering nutrients that
float down from above.

Near Antarctica the current
splits in two. Eventually both
currents rise up to the sunlit
surface water, bringing the
nutrients to the phytoplankton
that feed all ocean life.

My heat warms the
currents. Falling rain
dilutes their salty water.

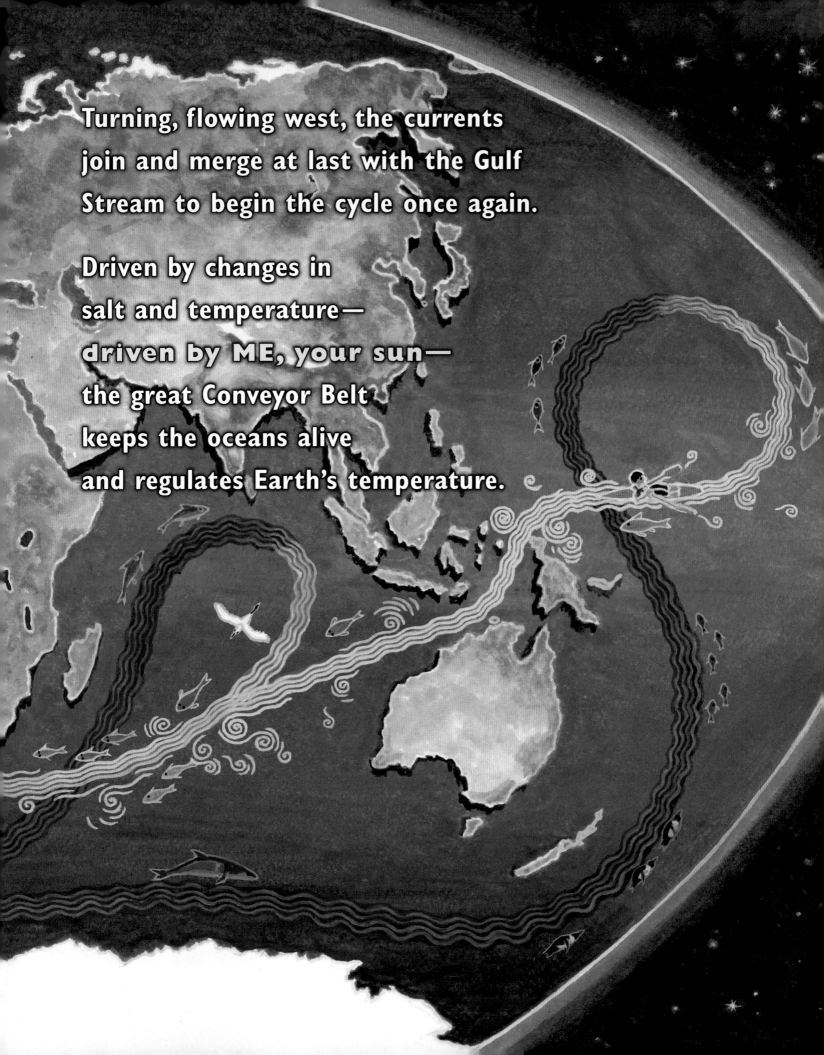

Turning, flowing west, the currents
join and merge at last with the Gulf
Stream to begin the cycle once again.

Driven by changes in
salt and temperature—
driven by ME, your sun—
the great Conveyor Belt
keeps the oceans alive
and regulates Earth's temperature.

Yes, my sunlight energy keeps water
moving around the planet—in the seas,
the sky, and the land, bringing your world to life.

Moving water also changes Earth's landscape.
Drop by drop, water can eat into hard rock.
Over eons, it carves deep canyons in the land.

As it flows over rocks, water pulls out essential
minerals—nutrients—delivering them to
all living things, including YOU.

Water seeps into cracks and freezes, breaking boulders into bits, carrying the rubble down, down, to the plains. Huge glaciers—rivers of frozen water—gouge deep valleys out of towering mountains.

Water is soft and yielding, but very powerful!

For billions of years, I, your sun, have cycled water around Earth as your ancestors made their homes near lakes and rivers so they would have enough water.

They built great civilizations by inventing waterworks—

digging wells and constructing dams, canals, and
aqueducts to control the flow of water.
As their populations grew, the water could feed
larger and larger
crops, and bigger
herds of animals.

The total amount of water on your Earth will always be the same. But now, more than seven billion people live on Earth, pouring wastes into rivers, lakes, and coastal waters, using and moving too much water. Some rivers are running dry. Some aquifers are being drained faster than rain can replenish them.

The water balance around the world is changing.

More and more places have too little water:
Drought dries up the crops.

More places have
too much: Floods
sweep over the land.

As your Earth warms, the
balance will shift even more. Sea
levels will rise, swamping coastal cities.

THIS I PROMISE:

I, your sun, will do my part
to keep Earth's water
clean and flowing.

Will you do your part?
Will you find ways to use water
sparingly and keep it clean?

REMEMBER:

You share Earth's
water with everything alive,
and your life depends on
the whole web of life.

NOTES ABOUT THIS BOOK

WATER IS LIFE.

We live on one special planet. Other planets have ice or water vapor, and some even appear to have oceans below their surface. But only Earth is covered with vast expanses of liquid water. Along with our 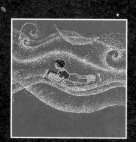 Goldilocks distance from the sun, this liquid water is what makes life-as-we-know-it possible.

It's not just the *presence* of water that gives Earth life. It's the fact that it is *constantly moving*: evaporating from the salty sea into fresh water, moving through the sky toward land, falling as rain or snow, seeping into groundwater, gathering into rivers, and finally, finally, flowing back into the sea. This global hydrological cycle is the focus of our story.

WATER, WATER, EVERYWHERE . . .

The total amount of water on our planet— about 332,000,000 cubic miles—has stayed the same for millions of years. While that sounds like a lot, if Earth were the size of an apple, and all that water was spread over its surface, it would form a film thinner than  the apple's skin! Almost 98 percent of Earth's water is saltwater in the oceans. Much of what's left—Earth's fresh water—is locked up in ice caps and glaciers, or groundwater. So only a tiny fraction of Earth's total water supply is readily available to life on Earth.

These numbers tell us *how much* water exists in different places, but not how fast it moves from place to place. This is the key to understanding water supply. Imagine yourself as the average water molecule moving through the global cycle. You will spend thousands of years in the ocean before you evaporate, and then ride with the wind for a few days before falling as rain or snow. If you fall into a lake, you will spend a few decades there; if into a river, or onto soil, you will stay there a few months. And if perchance a living creature swallows you, you will occupy its body for a few days before you move on. But if you seep into an aquifer, you could stay there for thousands of years, and if you end up frozen in Antarctica, you could stay there for hundreds of thousands of years. These  time frames are called residence times, and they reflect how long it takes to completely replace the water in a particular place with new water. Think of a deep aquifer full of contaminants. If the residence time there is short, the aquifer can be flushed clean quickly. But if it is long, the contaminants would stay there for a very long time.

WATER IS AN EXTRAORDINARY MOLECULE!

Water molecules are made of two hydrogen atoms attached to one oxygen atom in the middle—H_2O. Because of its special molecular structure, water is the only molecule known to exist as a solid, a liquid, and a gas (water vapor) at everyday pressures and temperatures.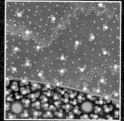

Individual water molecules can loosely attach to one another in many different ways. This enables water to hold a **LOT** of heat before its temperature increases—roughly ten times more than rocks, for example. This is why surface ocean currents can grab the sun's heat at the equator and carry it northward without

increasing in temperature so much as to kill all its inhabitants. Because of these special properties that water has—its ability to morph from liquid to solid to gas, and its heat capacity—water can move around the Earth, carrying the sun's heat with it.

Why don't lakes freeze to the bottom? Why does ice float? It's because of another bizarre feature of water. Like other liquids, water increases in density—weight per unit volume—as it cools. So in autumn, as surface lake waters cool, they sink to the bottom and fill the whole lake with cool, dense water. However, as winter approaches, and the surface water begins to freeze, that icy water starts to get lighter. Why? Because near the freezing point, the attachments between water molecules switch from a random to a regular pattern—a rigid structure

that has fewer molecules per unit volume (it's less dense) than liquid water. So ice floats above the slightly warmer (denser!) water below.

When water evaporates from any liquid surface (or from YOU, when you sweat), it changes from a liquid to water vapor, which is invisible. In the process, it takes some heat with it, cooling the surface it leaves, in what is called evaporative cooling. As warm water vapor rises in the atmosphere, it cools and eventually

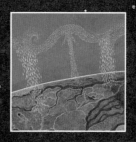

condenses as water droplets that form clouds and rain. The evaporation of water near the surface, followed by its recondensation high in the atmosphere, plays an important role in cooling the Earth's surface.

WATER IS A GREENHOUSE GAS—IT HELPS MAINTAIN EARTH'S TEMPERATURE.

In addition to helping cool the planet during the day, water also helps it stay warm at night. Water vapor is the largest contributor to the "greenhouse effect" that warms the Earth and regulates its temperature. How does this "cocoon," as we call it in our story, work? During the day, sunlight passes through the atmosphere and warms Earth's surface. The Earth releases this heat throughout the day, but more so at night when the air is cooler. Some

of that heat is trapped by the water vapor in the atmosphere and held there. Without water vapor and other greenhouse gases in our atmosphere, Earth's temperature would be 60°F cooler than it is today.

Water vapor not only controls the temperature of the Earth through its greenhouse properties, but the amount of water vapor is also *controlled by* temperature. As the Earth warms, more water evaporates, and water vapor in the atmosphere increases. Logically, then, one would think that warming would cause more warming. Then why hasn't the Earth just gotten warmer and warmer? Clouds! When air gets saturated with water, the vapor condenses into clouds whose white surfaces reflect sunlight back into space. This has a cooling effect that counteracts the greenhouse warming effect. Understanding the precise balance between these two forces is a major challenge for climate scientists as they try to understand the role of carbon dioxide released from fossil fuel burning in greenhouse warming (see our book *Buried Sunlight*).

WATER NOT ONLY KEEPS US HYDRATED — IT IS THE SPARK PLUG OF LIFE.

If we don't drink water, we die. But our dependency on water is even more fundamental than that. Water is *the* first molecule used by plants when they convert solar energy to chemical energy in photosynthesis. As we describe in our book *Living Sunlight*, in photosynthesis, plants gather the sun's energy  to split apart water, H_2O. Oxygen is released, and plants use the hydrogen atoms to build sugar out of carbon dioxide, CO_2. Then plants convert the sugar into molecules that build the plants' bodies. <u>This plant matter is the food that sustains the biosphere.</u> For every molecule of water that is split apart in photosynthesis, another is put back together through the respiration of animals that have eaten the plants, and by the plants themselves. This cycle keeps the molecules of life in balance. Although just a tiny, tiny fraction of all Earth's water goes through this water-to-water life cycle each year, that critical fraction is supplied by the constantly moving global cycle of water.

DURING PHOTOSYNTHESIS, PLANTS PUMP WATER INTO THE AIR.

Life itself helps keep water moving around the Earth. In order to photosynthesize, plants and trees have to open up tiny pores—stomata—

on their leaves so they can draw in CO_2 from the air. The opening of the pores allows water to escape—creating a vacuum of sorts, pulling more water from the soil through the plant's roots and up and out through the stomata—a process called *transpiration*. A large tree can transport nearly 100 gallons of water from the soil to the atmosphere each day; an acre of crops can send up thousands of gallons. All told, transpiration accounts for 10 percent of the flow of water into the atmosphere globally.

GIANT CURRENTS SUSTAIN OCEAN LIFE AND REGULATE OUR EARTH'S TEMPERATURE.

All of Earth's oceans are connected through massive currents. This global "ocean conveyer belt" keeps water moving from basin to basin and mixes it from surface to deep. As we describe in our book *Ocean Sunlight*, as this massive current moves along the sunlit ocean surface, its phytoplankton inhabitants photosynthesize, filling the water with oxygen. Eventually, the water sinks and delivers that oxygen to the creatures all along the ocean floor. Along the way, it collects "marine snow"—poop, parts of dead organisms, or pieces of gelatinous animals—falling from above. The "snow" particles decay and release nutrients into the deep-sea water. When the conveyer belt returns to the surface, the nutrients feed the phytoplankton, and all life that depends on them, once again.

The global conveyer belt does much more than sustain life in the oceans.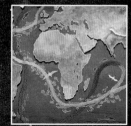

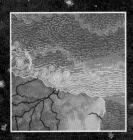

Driven by gradients in temperature and salt content, it plays a central role in redistributing heat around the globe. The circulation pattern is *much* more complex than we have depicted in the book, but the general principles are as follows: Surface waters that have been warmed near the equator carry their heat northward. They let go of it as they cool, warming the air. In the far north the water cools even more. Some freezes and squeezes out its salt; strong winds drive evaporation, making the water even saltier.

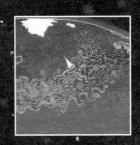

The very cold, very salty water sinks, and surface water rushes in to replace it. This drives a massive current flowing southward, deep inside the sea. As the current flows around Antarctica, it cools and sinks again, reenergized to continue on its journey. Ultimately this

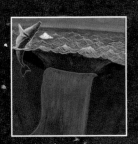

water rises up to the surface in far-distant places where it can be rewarmed by the sun, freshened by the rain, and move on. The journey of a water parcel through the entire circuit takes about a thousand years. Collectively, the circulation of the conveyer belt tempers the climate of the whole Earth by redistributing heat from the equator to the poles.

WATER SHAPES THE SURFACE OF THE EARTH AND DELIVERS ESSENTIAL MINERALS TO ALL LIFE.

Water is powerful. Look at the great canyons, carved by the steady flow of water over eons, or at sandy beaches, each grain sculpted by the

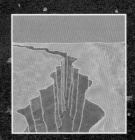

endless pounding of waves. Even solid water in the form of glaciers has the power to gouge enormous valleys, such as those in the Alps and Rocky Mountains. Slowly, relentlessly, the glaciers gnaw away at solid rock. And repeated cycles of freezing and thawing allow water trapped in cracks of rocks to split the rocks wide open. Finally, as water flows over rocks and through the soil, it dissolves essential minerals, making them available to plants and animals. Just as

your blood—which is 92 percent water— carries nutrients throughout your body, water carries the nutrients needed by all living things on Earth, continuously renewing them.

BEAVERS ARE NATURE'S ECOSYSTEM ENGINEERS!

Although we did not have room to describe this in our story, beavers are impressive hydrological engineers! Before the fur trade decimated beaver populations far and wide, the dams built by those hundreds of millions of beavers controlled a large percentage of the waterways from the Canadian Arctic to northern Mexico. Some estimates suggest that one-tenth of the entire land area of the US—including some of the now-arid western regions—was once covered by ponds and wetlands created by beavers. These were habitats for diverse species of plants and animals and provided drought insurance by stabilizing the water table. Furthermore, when beavers abandoned their homes and moved on, the silt and nutrients collected by their dams spread over the land and created fertile "beaver meadows" for diverse species of plants.

The near extinction of the beaver by the fur trade changed irreversibly the way watersheds functioned across the US and Canada. Thanks to conservation efforts beginning in the early 1800s, beaver numbers have rebounded. Wildlife managers know how to coax them to

build dams where they will create desired ponds and wetlands. These efforts have been so successful in restoring ecosystems that beavers are being reintroduced in areas of the Southwest for this purpose. Ecosystem restoration at its best!

HUMANS AND THE WATER CYCLE

Like the beaver, humans have changed the paths of water for thousands of years to serve our needs. We keep learning what works and what doesn't. While dams supply us with power and help control floods, many have become obsolete and too expensive to maintain.

We have begun to take some dams down, recognizing that the ecosystem services of the natural habitat sometimes have a higher value. We have put the meanders back into some of the rivers we once straightened, restoring their valuable habitats.

We are also learning that the rates at which we are drawing water from some aquifers are not sustainable. We are draining them dry, and the land above them is collapsing to fill the void. Much of the water we use is for agriculture, and a huge fraction of it goes toward the production of animal protein. A serving of meat requires roughly 500 times more water to produce than a serving of vegetable protein. So reducing our

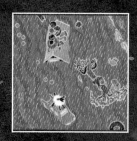

consumption of meat is one way we can help the global water problem. At the same time, we must work toward water management systems that use our growing understanding of local, national, and global water supplies, and advanced monitoring technologies, to design efficient and sustainable water systems. People living in different ecosystems have different problems with their water, from drought to floods to pollution to saltwater infiltration. What is important is to understand the local problems and take appropriate action.

WATER AND CLIMATE CHANGE

As we describe in our book *Buried Sunlight*, the steady increase in atmospheric CO_2 over the past century is most likely causing significant global warming. As we describe above, like CO_2, water is also a greenhouse gas, and it is an extremely important component of models designed to predict future climate scenarios. Warming caused by burning fossil fuels will increase evaporation rates, which will lead to more water vapor, potentially adding to the greenhouse-warming effect of elevated CO_2.

A warmer Earth results in warmer seas, and because water expands—gets less dense—as it warms, sea levels will rise. A warmer Earth melts polar ice sheets, causing sea levels to rise even more. There is evidence that the influx of fresh meltwater into the North Atlantic is

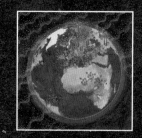

causing a decrease in salinity. Will this lowered salinity slow down the ocean conveyor belt? A sluggish conveyor belt could have far-reaching consequences for the distribution of heat around the Earth.

These are just a few of the many complex feedback loops that connect Earth's temperature, the water cycle, sea levels, and the greenhouse effect. This complexity makes the prediction of future climate scenarios very difficult. One thing is certain, however: Understanding the water cycle is central to forecasting climate change.

IMPORTANT THINGS ABOUT WATER THAT WE LEFT OUT OF THIS BOOK

It does not matter how much water we have if it is not free of toxins and pathogens. This is an enormous dimension of the global water problem. As the saying goes, "We are all downstream." This problem is so complex that it would need another book to begin to address it.

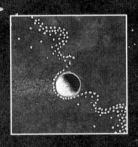

Finally, we left out one major movement of water for lack of space: tidal motion. Here we must give our moon some credit! While the gravitational pull of the sun plays a role in the daily rise and fall of sea level due to the tides, the gravitational pull of the moon is much stronger because of its proximity to Earth. As the Earth moves around the sun, the moon is orbiting us, and together their pull causes the oceans to bulge in complex and interesting ways. The net effect is the ever-variable, always-present tides.

THE NEXT TIME YOU DRINK A GLASS OF WATER, remember this: All those water molecules have been constantly moving, through sea and sky, lakes and streams, through plants and worms, insects and

elephants—giving them life. Where might those molecules go next as they leave your body and move on? What are ALL the ways those molecules sustain life on Earth and shape the very nature of our blue planet?

TREASURE

YOUR WATER;

IT IS YOUR LIFE.

Thanks go to Rogier Braakman, Dara Entekhabi, Mick Follows, Jim Green, Dennis McLaughlin, Robert Pickart, and Steve Rintoul for their help.
—M.B. & P.C.

THE BLUE SKY PRESS

Published by The Blue Sky Press, an imprint of Scholastic Inc., *Publishers since 1920.* SCHOLASTIC, THE BLUE SKY PRESS, and associated logos are trademarks and/or registered trademarks of Scholastic Inc.

Library of Congress catalog card number: 2015031582
ISBN 978-0-545-80541-4
10 9 8 7 6 5 4 3 2 1   17 18 19 20 21
Printed in China   38

This book was printed on paper containing 50% post-consumer waste recycled materials.
First edition, February 2017
Designed by Kathleen Westray